The Revenge of the Child

Thoughts on How to Prevent

Future Holocausts from the

Thoughts of Chandra Lal (Tom Pierce)

Order this book online at www.trafford.com
or email orders@trafford.com

Most Trafford titles are also available at major online book retailers.

Printed in Victoria, BC, Canada.

ISBN: 978-1-4269-1661-8 (soft)
ISBN: 978-1-4269-1662-5 (hard)

Library of Congress Control Number: 2010901043

Our mission is to efficiently provide the world's finest, most comprehensive book publishing service, enabling every author to experience success. To find out how to publish your book, your way, and have it available worldwide, visit us online at www.trafford.com

Trafford rev. 1/27/2010

 www.trafford.com

North America & international
toll-free: 1 888 232 4444 (USA & Canada)
phone: 250 383 6864 ♦ fax: 812 355 4082

TABLE OF CONTENTS

III

Dedication

To the children of the world

In spirit and in age

And to the one great generation

Which will break

The Chain-of-Darkness

My Cry

I speak for those

Whose only voice

Is a cry of pain

And rage

Hear me –

For without your hearing them

There is no future

Not for you

Nor me, nor anyone –

In all the earth.

THREE PURPOSES

Purpose I

The purpose of this book is to prevent, in so far as possible, avenging actions by one – or a few persons who seek revenge against society – or some group in society. Ours is an age of micro-miniaturization together with atomic and biological weaponry. Danger to a part of society is a threat to all in our world.

Purpose II

To break forever the "Chain of Darkness," the generation-to-generation continuation of child abuse, will greatly lessen the suffering in our world. It is also the only way that Purpose I can be accomplished.

Purpose III

That which is most precious is the child.

This child has become each one of us.

Because of this, what each one does affects the entire world.

Accordingly, each one has a part or share in the responsibility for the entire world.

X

ACKNOWLEDGEMENTS

1. To put into one paragraph the values and blessings of a lifetime friendship is indeed a good challenge. I have known Dr. Kurt von Syppli Kynell since 1939. He has been a most kind and helpful friend and supporter since those days of Junior High School in Long Beach, California. After careers in the United States Navy in WW II and later in the Sheriff's Department of Los Angeles County, he took up the academic life with a B.A. and M.A. from Stanford and later a Ph.D. from Carnegie-Mellon University. At the end of his teaching career, he received the title of Professor Emeritus. He is the author of three books:

A Different Frontier – Alaska Criminal Justice, 1935 – 1965

One Man's Nagasaki: A Personal Sea Odyssey

Saxon and Medieval Antecedents of the English Common Law

He is currently doing research in Europe for an intellectual and psychological biography of Gottfried Wilhelm von Leibnetz. Our time together has shown that a true friendship can grow not just through years, but through decades.

2. It is from reading Dr. Alice Miller's famous book "For Your Own Good" that I began to have a series of insights about child abuse in general and

Adolph Hitler in particular. Her factual action-reaction approach, in contrast to the abstract psychoanalytic one so often encountered, has been of tremendous help. For some years, I wondered and researched the question of what could cause such implacable hatred. Her writings have much value in our present situation as she understands the generation-to-generation continuity of child abuse which I have called "The Chain of Darkness."

3. In the process of research for this volume, I soon began to wonder if could go further than two centuries back in terms of the child-abuse part of the total milieu. I was delighted to find that this was indeed possible; much further than I had first thought. Dr. James De Meo's book "Saharasia" has not only provided an unlikely synthesis of Climatology and Cultural Anthropology, but has shown that the "Chain-of-Darkness" is some 6,000 years old. I am deeply grateful for Dr. De Meo's fine work.

4. To Bonnie Kelly, whose flying fingers and keen insight have translated my handwritten version into electronic and hard-copy form, my deepest thanks.

Acknowledgment

It is with the most profound appreciation that I acknowledge the help provided by Dr. Morton Schatzman in his book <u>Soul Murder, Persecution in the Family</u>(Allen Lane, a Division of Penguin Books, Ltd.21 John Street, London WCI; ISBN 0-7139-0321-X)
Various factors: societal, economical, political, and historical were involved but it is only by understanding the psychological factors, the destructive revenging motivation arising from child abuse, that one may see how the series of horrors actually came about.
Dr. Schatzman's book clearly deliniates how the child raising system in vogue in Germany at the time that the generation which became the NAZIS was being raised actually created the reaction to the abuse. This reaction was the holocaust.

Again referring to the son's "revelations," Canetti says:

> As no-one today is likely to deny, his [Schreber's, the son's] political system had within a few decades been accorded high honour: though in a rather cruder and less literate form it became the creed of a great nation, leading . . . to the conquest of Europe and coming within a hair's breadth of the conquest of the world. Thus Schreber's claims were posthumously vindicated by his unwitting disciples. We are not likely to accord him the same recognition, but the amazing and incontrovertible likeness between the two systems may serve to justify the time we have devoted to this single case of paranoia. . . .
> (p. 447)

Ritter, writing about Dr. Schreber, the father, in 1936, saw in him a spiritual precursor of Nazism. Ritter admired both Dr. Schreber and Hitler.

Anyone who wishes to understand German "character structure" in the Nazi era could profitably study Dr. Schreber's books.

There are many passages in Hitler's *Mein Kampf* (1939) that resemble Dr. Schreber's views. Hitler, like Dr. Schreber, abhors what he calls weakness, cowardice, laziness, softness, and indolence. He speaks, as Dr. Schreber does, of the "moral and physical decadence" of his time (p. 352).

Hitler, like Dr. Schreber, demands compliance with parts of his *own* mind he calls the Divine Will and Nature; Nature, for Hitler, is the "ruthless Queen of Wisdom" (p. 124). Hitler condemns pre-Nazi society for committing sins "against the image of God" (p. 352). Hitler and Dr. Schreber urge obedience to what they must experience as overwhelming powers: "God," "Fate," "Necessity," and "History." These indeterminate abstractions are, in fact, names for programs governing *their* minds. Hitler and Dr. Schreber, in pretending to derive from them authority over others, are also submitting to them themselves. The control they impose upon others is the control that controls themselves.

XIV

Figure 1 (p. 197) The "bridge." Dr. Schreber thought a forward slump of a child's head and shoulders when walking was "a clear expression of weakness, dumbness and cowardice." He devised the "bridge," an exercise "to strengthen the back and neck muscles" of children who slumped.

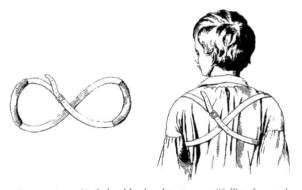

Figure 2 (p. 198) A shoulder band to prevent "falling forward of the shoulders." Dr. Schreber thought it should be worn every day, all day, until "the bad habit is regulated." The shaded parts of the band on the left are metal springs to rest on the front of the shoulders.

172

XV

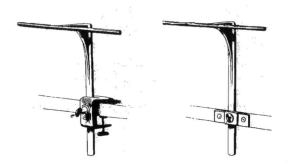

Figure 3 (p. 203) The Geradhalter. On the left is a portable
one for home use. The one on the right was fixed to desks at
school.

Figure 4 (p. 205) The Geradhalter in use.

nine by nature and attitude that sober reasoning determines their thoughts and actions far less than emotion and feeling . . ." MEIN KAMPF

It is not a matter of being that way "by nature" but of being a typical example of the reproduction of an authoritarian social system in the structures of its members. (1946, pp. 44–45)

Of course. Despotism at any level—state, factory, school, church, family, individual—breeds and needs despotism at all levels.

Later Reich writes:

German fascism was born from the biological rigidity and crippling of the former generation. Prussian militarism, with its machine-like discipline, its goose-step, its "belly in, chest out!" is the extreme manifestation of this biological rigidity . . . It is clear: social freedom and self-regulation are inconceivable in rigid, machine-like people. (*Ibid.*, p. 301)

Dr. Schreber's exercises in obedience and stiff posture had given some Prussian soldiers their basic training from infancy.

Hitler talks of training children in erect posture:

In the People's State the army will no longer be obliged to teach boys how to walk and stand erect. . . . (1939, p. 358)

The army will no longer need to because families and especially schools will already have done the job.

A cost of training soldiers from babyhood may be that some babies go mad later on. A good or a bad bargain according to one's values.

173

XVII

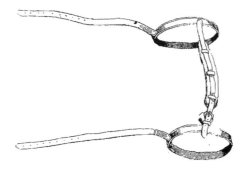

Figure 5 (p. 174) A belt for the sleeping child.

Figure 6 (174) The belt in use.

Figure 7 (p. 199)
The Kopfhalter.

Figure 8 (p. 220)
The chin band.

INTRODUCTION

At the beginning of a new century which is also the start of a new millennium, it is very appropriate to consider the high and low points of the 20th century.

The two high points are: (1) the discovery of cold fusion and (2) the Marshall Plan for European recovery after WW II. The two low points are: (1) the atomic bombing of Hiroshima and Nagasaki and (2) the Holocaust in Europe.

In view of the large and still growing historical and interpretive literature relating to the Hitlerian-era and WW II, it was my particular interest and concern to work with the ideas which constitute this book.

The present time (2002) provides an illustration of the fact that the same destructive forces as those present in 1939-1945 are still operating in our home-world. One has only to see TV reports from Rawanda and Bosnia, later Serbia and Kosovo.

Human progress is dependent on human understanding. To make, by inspiration, insight, and creativity, a contribution to mass understanding is a signal honor and blessing.

The battle between the constructive forces of light and the destructive forces of darkness in the human psyche is older than recorded history.

Today, thanks to improved communication, we have a global village where the blessings or curses received by one are known to all. This means, among other things, that each one has the right to the protection and help of all. Mass understanding of this right is _slowly_ increasing.

That correct application of understanding will improve our world-home and the lives and conditions of all is as certain as the sun rising in the east. That lack of application will fail to help us all is as equally certain.

The mass consciousness, armed with understanding, and aided by action, can transform our world-home to a far safer, cleaner, and more beautiful place for us all.

At the present moment in history, — 57 years after the end of the Hitlerian Holocaust, there have been very many books, articles, and analyses (both from an historical perspective and from psychological perspectives) of WW II and the war within a war (which the holocaust was).

It might appear because of the above that for an author to add to the abundance of extant material by one more book would be at his/her peril.

My reply to this is:

(1)　To the best of my knowledge, with all that could be discovered by research, there is no overall synthesis of the factors (historical and psychological) which presents

2

a complete comprehensive explanation of the events in

Europe from 1918 through 1945.

(2)   Ever since the end of the Holocaust in 1945, the cry has

been heard "Never again!," but no one has any ideas of

how this may be accomplished.

Statement of General Principles Considered

Revenge and the misuse of power which so often
accompanies it, has been long noted in human history.
(Reference 1) – As long as these capacities remain in the
human psyche and are not recognized, understood, and
constructively re-directed, there will be colossal and
preventable tragedies.

Since the end of WW II in 1945, there has been a series of outbreaks

of violence of mankind against itself.

These include:

Zaire

Cambodia (Reference 3)

Bosnia

Serbia vs Albania (Kosovo)

In all of these, the Barbaric Pattern of Conquest noted in my book,

"Brotherhood or Extinction" (Reference 4) could be easily seen.

(3)   The present situation is so precarious and dangerous that

immediate understanding and action is needed.

3

(4)   It is my trust in providing this explanation that

motivation for action will arise and overcome the inertia

of procrastination and hypocrisy which only permits the

present dire situation to become more painful for some

and more dangerous for all.

PART I

WWW

What Went Wrong in Germany

Between 1918 and 1945

PART I

TABLE OF CONTENTS

5

Section C – Definitions of Terms Used
Six Essential Chapters

Chapter 1. Child Abuse
Types of Child Abuse:
    VI. Physical
    VII. Emotional
    VIII. Sexual
    IX. Psychological
    X.   Exploitation
The Foundation of Personality

Chapter 2. The Results of Child Abuse
    Positive and Negative
    Energy Expression
    The Child's View of Abuse

Chapter 3. Child Rearing

Chapter 4. Bonding

Chapter 5. Empowerment
    C. Dis-Empowerment
    D. Re-Empowerment

Chapter 6. Revenge
    Revenge and Forgiveness
    9. Hope
    10. Love
    11. Projection
    12. Blame
    13. Control
    14. Charisma
    15. Domination
    16. Interiorization

References Cited in Part I

SECTION A

OBJECTIVE

The Average Objective Experience of the Average German Citizen in the period 1918 through 1945.

Part 1. Social, Economic, and Political Issues, Blame, and the Conflict of Groups

In the years from 1918 through 1932, the citizens of Germany experienced an interaction of social, economic, and political forces which could, at best, be called chaotic. On January 30, 1933, Hitler became Chancellor and the social and economic situation stabilized at the expense of all freedom for Germany. (Reference 6, pg. 217)

Germany was a defeated nation, forced by the Treaty of Versailles to pay 132 billion gold marcs in reparations, but without the economic capacity to produce any such value; the bill presented by the Allied powers in April, 1921 only added to the stress on the Weimar Republic. (Reference 2)

Under the force of (1) unemployment and (2) uncontrolled inflation, social conditions deteriorated to the point that middle-class families prostituted their own daughters. (Reference 5)

A series of crises ensued: 1919, 1920, and 1923. All these helped the NAZI cause; then came the worldwide depression of 1929 which gave a great boost to their plans and power. (Reference 2, pg. 23)

Part 3.   Unemployment

From 1918 to 1928, unemployment was always over 1 million. In 1928, it was 650,000. With the coming of the Depression of October 24, 1929, millions lost their jobs. (Reference 2, pg. 24)

Part 4.   Uncontrolled Inflation

Most history students know the stories of a wheelbarrow full of marks needed to buy a stamp or a loaf of bread. In January, 1923 the mark was 10,000 per dollar; in June, it was 150,000. Currency in circulation was 44 trillion marks. (Reference 5, pg. 72)

From 1914 to 1918, the amount of money in circulation was five times as great. (Reference 9, pg. 435) WW I was financed by loans, not taxes.

SECTION B

SUBJECTIVE

The Average Subjective Experience of the Average German Citizen in the period 1918 through 1945.

The psychological effects of severe child abuse.

Every child entering this world comes here seeking (A) physical nursing and (B) physical and psychological support and help. Years of patient devoted work are necessary to guide the newly arrived soul through the stages of infancy, toddler, childhood, and adolescence. We may ask, "Why has nature made the path so difficult and complex?" The answer is that each child has something unique to give to the world.

To block the expression of this gift by abuse is the greatest of crimes because it (1) is the greatest injury to the child and (2) is the cause of all crimes against the world.

The child, seeking love and support, and finding hate and pain, goes through a series of stages.

Subconscious Volume

There comes a time when the subconscious volume of resulting rage takes over the subconscious mind and increasingly controls the conscious mind. This results in the removal of any feelings of kindness or mercy. It also unleashes the maximum possible destructive force within the child if turned inward or the destruction of all nearby (or further) if turned outward.

FEAR   Progressive insanity

SORROW

GRIEF

DEPRESSION

DESPAIR

RAGE

11

SECTION C

Definitions of Terms Used

Six Essential Chapters

CHAPTER 1

Child Abuse

Types of Child Abuse

I. Physical

Shaking

Beating (including spanking)

Whipping

Burning

Scalding

Starving

Physical Dangers

Etc.

N. B. Changing the name (beating/spanking) does not change

the pain/insult received by the child

II. Emotional

A. Self-image destruction

1) Verbal

"You're no good —"

"You'll never be anything —"

etc.

12

2) Lack of needed help and support (encouragement)

B. Lack of Ethical Training

This results in poor or no relationships.

III. Sexual

Rape

Incest

Shaming

Accusation

Making natural functions (masturbation or elimination)

unnatural

IV. Psychological

Parents not able themselves to become figure skaters, acrobats, or star athletes project these careers on their children; in this way living through the child what they could (or did) not do themselves. Each child is entitled to *her/his own career*; the gift they came to give to the world.

V. Exploitation

Under this heading comes child labor in many countries, and an especially flagrant case by the United States of America. Please

13

refer to Peter Jennings excellent documentary on Saipan aired on PBS-TV in 1998 and 1999.

The Foundation of Personality

The foundation of the personality of each child born on earth is formed NOT by the:

Parents

Caregivers

Siblings

Relatives

Peers

School

Society

BUT by the type and amounts of child abuse received or NOT received.

Child abuse not received constitutes support for the child in her/his entire life.

Child abuse received constitutes NON-support for her/his entire life.

CHAPTER 2

The Results of Child Abuse

Psychological

The psychological effects of child abuse are the responses of each child to the various types of pain, insult, and invasion received. These responses are:

HATE

FEAR

RAGE

Parents, peers, teachers, and society demand that the child NOT act out these feelings. What happens to the energy, the psychological power of the response? It is stored in the psychological make-up of the child on an unconscious level. This stored energy affects all future behavior until it is released. The feelings/energy must be released in *some* way.

I. POSITIVE WAYS

Psychotherapy

Every approach and school of therapy will yield *some* benefit:

A. Verbal therapy

B. Somatically-oriented psychotherapy

C. G-Spot therapy

D. Rebirthing

E. Witnessing (subjective integration), etc.

II. NEGATIVE WAYS

A. CRIME (individual or organized)

The idea that "I/we can get away with _____."

B. REVENGE

The holocaust, the revenge of the children.

C. DISEASE

Long-term disease conditions in which the rage is directed inward.

The Child's View of Abuse

We are now able to consider the old and well-known phrase:

"Power corrupts - Absolute power corrupts absolutely."

in a new way.

I. Every child arrives totally helpless and powerless, seeking love by which to live.

II. All emotions, thoughts, and actions are based on one, and only one, of two factors or motivations: (1) love or (2) fear.

\7

III. The child, because of youth and size, has neither psychological nor mechanical defenses against abuse.

IV. The actions of abuse (physical, sexual, emotional, verbal, etc.) result in a state of total FEAR.

V. This fear is felt and understood by the child as a threat to SURVIVAL. This is the most basic of all threats for it means life versus death.

VI. The parent, or other abuser, because of maturity and size has ABSOLUTE power (life and death) over the child.

VII. The child, seeking love and life, has found in abuse, fear and the immediate threat of death.

VIII. At this early point in a new life, the child becomes aware of the total travesty of his or her present life.

IX. It is on this total travesty that the insanity of revenge is based.

Hitler's one goal was always absolute power, by which to accomplish total revenge. This was revenge against: (1) his father, (2) the Jews, and (3) the world. This process was well advanced, "Today Europe - Tomorrow the World," at the time of D-Day, June 6, 1944 when the world reversed it.

Interior Mechanism

Recent developments in psychiatric – theory/practice (TV – 20/20, 3-4-98) have shown that in cases of severe child abuse, it is possible for the individual to create multiple autonomous personalities. This is now called "Disassociative Identity Disorder (DID)." "A" may not know what "B" is doing. The energy which makes possible this disorder, if directed outward through blame projection ("US vs THEM"), could account for many of the horrors visited by the NAZI regime on the Jews and others in WW II.

Exterior Mechanism

Under the NAZI regime, the Gestapo (Secret Police) kept order and eliminated dissenters – usually by killing them.

The actual genocide in the concentration camps was carried out by a variety of means:

GASSING

POISON

BURNING TO DEATH

WORKING TO DEATH

"MEDICAL EXPERIMENTS"

Etc.

19

The Schützstaffel (SS) which grew from the 21 thugs, who initially formed Hitler's bodyguard, to over one million men, all dedicated by oath to fulfilling Hitler's will.

I. The younger the child, the more profound the effects which are produced.

II. The greater the intellectual potential, the greater the: (A) power of denial and (B) the greater the fantasy compensation.

III. If an opportunity later arises in the child's life to act out revenge/fantasy compensation, then these actions will show a maximum of creativity and horror.

IV. Patterns of response range from schizophrenic perceptual distortion where people are perceived as objects (and therefore burnable as fuel) to multiple personalities, each quite able to operate without any awareness of the others.

The process of the creation of multiple personalities happens when the child is rejected by the mother and the force behind the child (which may be called the soul) makes a series of attempts or personalities to overcome the mother's rejection and so be able to survive.

Seeking, Finding, and the Results

The child, seeking love for his/her arrival in our world, and finding abuse instead, soon comes to the conclusion that he/she is not WORTHY of love. This conclusion shatters the self-image of the child. The rebuilding of the self-image then involves the efforts of the child in therapy, bonding, or other activity for the rest of his/her lifetime.

The Division of Potential

Trauma of any sort results in emotional force becoming unconscious. This means that motivation cannot be at a normal maximum. The greater the trauma, the greater the amount of emotional force absorbed into the unconscious state. The greater the threat to life, the larger the amount of attention needed to survive.

Trauma is the enemy of self-esteem. Without self-esteem, the natural motivation toward accomplishment cannot be expressed as there is no worthy self to receive the benefits of the good work done.

Repeated trauma results in ever larger amounts of emotional force becoming transferred to unconsciousness. This means that the part of the personality that remains conscious has an ever decreasing amount of energy available with which to work. Because of this, frustration increases with each increase in the amount of trauma.

The Loss to Society

The present state of our culture and technology is the result of someone's flash of inspiration or insight, multiplied by the number of geniuses and inventors. One of the prime results of child abuse is continuing emotional problems. These emotional problems prevent the inspiration or insight being completed and given to the world. Everyone has SOMETHING to give, great or small.

If the giving is prevented by the continuing emotional struggle, then the loss is to the entire world.

There is no definite way to tell what this loss may be. Another Di Vinci, Mozart, or Einstein?

22

CHAPTER 3

Child Rearing

In beginning courses in psychology, it is noted that the child at first

has only two fears: falling and loud noises. In the case of the abused child,

there is a third fear. This is the fear of non-survival. Being:

>Small

>Alone

>Abused

>Without physical support, and

>Without psychological support (bonding)

is a terrifying situation.

As the growth process continues, denial may keep the remnants of the

original personality together. However, DENIAL DOES NOT HEAL, it

only suppresses the memory of the pain of the abuse. The pain and the

desperate need for re-empowerment continue as subconscious forces.

Evidence of the degree of desperation in the search for re-

empowerment and bonding may be found in the history of the Ahnenerbe,

the NAZI Occult Bureau. (Reference 11)

CHAPTER 4

Bonding

"Bonding" is defined for our purposes here as "psychic bonding", a subtle, powerful sense of mutual concern and support, a sense of mutual love such as ideally occurs between parents and children, and between siblings. It can also be defined as the sense of brotherly/sisterly concern and the unity of purpose found in fraternal orders.

The NAZI party bonded destructively, this was ALL THEY HAD.

The foundation of the process of socialization is, and indeed must be, the bonds formed between the child and 1) parents, 2) siblings, 3) teachers, and 4) peers. If there is an interference with the bonding process, then socialization will be correspondingly distorted or even missing.

The remainder of the child's personality will seek through collective means what was denied on an individual basis. This is group bonding and group action based on group experience and needs.

The maximum power of the bonding process occurs when those who bond are jointly the survivors of difficult or threatening experiences. This happened with (1) Hitler and those who experienced economic problems and (2) Hitler and those who experienced child abuse.

It also occurred within the German people as a whole, awaiting only the galvanizing/unifying effect of the appearance of a leader who would bring hope.

The Application of Psychological Principles

There are two sets of principles which apply in the two cases of the abused and the normal unabused child:

THE ABUSED CHILD	THE NORMAL CHILD
CAUSE	CAUSE
Unloving, uncaring destructive environment	Loving, supportive environment
RESULT	RESULT
Lack of bonding due to FEAR OF BONDING	Bonding with parents and later with peers and teachers.
FURTHER RESULT	Trusting the environment,
The child feels that his/her Survival is only possible by his/her control (destructive control) of the environment.	he/she works _with_ the environment.

ABUSED ADULTS	NORMAL ADULT
RESULT	RESULT
Crime from destructive	Creative work yields benefits
control costs many billions	to all.
of dollars, spent needlessly.	

Gangs and Crime – Bonding in the Negative Sense – "Gang-Related" Crime

Mutual strength can be gained by bonding with one's peers. The "feedback" which happens in any project, constructive or destructive (revengeful) is helpful to the project. Together with this is the addition of mutual emotional support. This is a very great help to the project.

A person who feels dis-empowered because of his/her history of abuse will often join destructively-oriented groups or "gangs." Each person will then be able to contribute his/her feedback/ingenuity to the gang which will enhance its destructive capacity.

The repressive reaction of society, and its arm — the police, is not considered. This is true because (1) the motivation of revenge is so great and (2) there is no instruction in ethics in the early grades of our school system.

If there is no deep intra-family bonding, then there is a great danger of the person becoming a member of a gang.

26

By noting the lives, words, and actions of friends who have

experienced severe child abuse; and also having taken graduate-level courses

in the psychology of child abuse and child development, there have been

some general conclusions reached about some of the ranges of effects which

happen to those who experience child abuse.

Without bonding, the preciousness of life cannot be recognized.

The abused child *cannot* bond with the abuser; and therefore, wishes

that the abuser had chosen abortion; and/or infanticide.

An unbonded generation will have no regard for life. This was the

generation which became the NAZIS.

OUTSIDE — CHAOS

INSIDE — NO REGARD FOR LIFE

TOGETHER — REVENGE

Hitler's bonding was with the (subjective) destructive aspect of the

abused German people together with the charisma which he used with such

efficiency to direct his own desire for revenge against the Jews, Europe, and

(planned) the world.

There are other possibilities (sources) of Hitler's charisma.

See Part II.

The need for bonding is so great that those without it are willing to undergo additional pain to bond as a group. (Reference 11)

"The Master Race" – Re-empowerment by Bonding

This is well illustrated by the present street and school violence in America. Children of close families with loving bonds have no need to become gang members. Instead they become martyrs and victims of those WITHOUT loving bonds at home who must act out their need for love and good bonding by street and school violence (drugs, drive-by shootings, and weapons at school).

CHAPTER 5

Empowerment

It is the sense of BEING ABLE TO DO a given action; mental, physical, emotional, or spiritual which can well be called "empowerment."

Without this sense of ability, inertia prevails and no action (on any level) is performed.

A. DIS-EMPOWERMENT

The dis-empowerment process from the viewpoint of the abused child:

I.   Less size and strength

II. Less acquainted with the world

III. To survive, the child is compelled to deny and make the experience unconscious.

IV. Psychic energy is needed to support denial and build psychic armor, so there is less energy available for living.

V.   Therefore ... the need for re-empowerment is URGENT.

Other results of abuse include patterns of emotionally caused action. These patterns are very resistant to change even after years of a variety of therapeutic approaches.

Abuse is the ultimate dis-empowering action. Children come here to do something. Abuse by dis-empowering prevents or delays this, so preventing or delaying the entire purpose of life.

B. RE-EMPOWERMENT

It is the sense of constructive re-empowerment that is sought by all the customers of the entire self-help psychology industry.

Books

Tapes

Videos

Seminars

Workshops

Meetings

Etc.

It is the feeling of CONCERN, bonding, that is the most powerful force available in the re-empowerment process.

CHAPTER 6

Revenge

For our purposes in this book, revenge is an action or actions, by an avenger (who earlier was a victim). This action or actions, serve in the mind and emotional state of the avenger, to compensate, pay back, settle, or balance the pain and difficulty given to the avenger when the avenger was a victim.

Revenge may be isolated or multiple. It may also be direct or _symbolic_. It may be done as part of some group action against another group for totally _symbolic_ reasons. The individual need for revenge may be somewhat reduced by actions taken in a group membership. This is especially true in cases where the avenger felt severely dis-empowered when he/she was a victim.

The greater the physical or emotional pain and difficulty received by the avenger, when a victim, the greater the pain and difficulty given to the NEW victim by the avenger. This applies (ideally for the avenger) mode for mode and type for type.

The entire force of evolution is directed toward individualized expression of ideas. Blocking this force by abuse produces rage and the NEED for revenge. Circumstances may produce, as it did with the NAZIS,

31

the opportunity for revenge. Going against this force due to dominance by another produces great unnecessary amounts of suffering. Individuality itself requires freedom. This is particularly the freedom of self-discovery and self-expression.

Revenge and Forgiveness

Revenge can only be a motivation if there is someone to do the avenging. This "someone" is the ego — the sense of separateness from other persons and all outwardly perceived things.

Forgiveness is a much rarer mental and spiritual capacity in which the mind relaxes, to some extent, its tight hold on the ideas of separateness and doership. Ultimate separateness comes from abuse.

So we have:

Degree of Separateness	Response to Injury
Ego	Revenge
Less ego	Forgiveness

1. Hope

Hope may be considered as the feeling that what is wanted/needed will happen. In post WW I Germany, so many factors were unstable; and interacting to produce additional

32

instability; that it was difficult to have faith in the possibility of improvement in even one aspect of life.

2. Love

To attempt to define love in words is completely useless, as intellectual comprehension is not possible. Love is none-the-less what everyone, human, animal, plant, and the earth itself is seeking.

Western philosophy says love or God, is:

OMNIPOTENT

OMNIESCIENT

OMNIPRESENT

Eastern philosophy say that Brahman, infinite spirit, can be experienced as:

SAT — inconceivable power

CHID — holy presence

ANANDA — bliss

Dr. Richard Bucke, in his synthesis of religious experiences, "COSMIC CONSCIOUSNESS" found God, love, as subjective light, moral elevation, and intellectual illumination. (Reference 12: The Man and the Book)

For the purposes of this book, love is kindness, patience, and support in child rearing.

3. Projection

Each person has the capacity to ascribe to another person or group, qualities or powers which they consciously or unconsciously have within themselves. These qualities or powers may be considered positive or negative. Projection is part of our psychic defense system. It is a way of decreasing internal stress if the quality or power is considered negative.

4. Blame

Blame is the assignment of responsibility for some negative action or result to another person or group. It results in a polarity; a sense of "us" (positive) versus "them" (negative). It is another way of decreasing internal stress.

5. Control

The person having "CONTROL" is the one who decides what happens to another person. This is without respect to the desires or interests of the other person.

Consider two identical cases:

    (1)   the child abuser and the child

    (2)   the guard and the concentration camp inmate

In both cases, the ultimate control is the power of life-or-death. Control reversed is *revenge*. Once control is reversed, there is no limit to the amount and variety of anger expressed.

6.   Charisma

Charisma is a charming aspect of personality which has the power to change the *belief structure* of others.

POSITIVE charisma makes for belief in TRUTH and leads to constructive action and freedom.

NEGATIVE charisma (equally charming) leads others to the belief in what is not true and the resulting destruction and enslavement.

Only ONE with charisma is needed to mobilize *all* and destroy many.

Hitler was favorable to being worshipped. He said there should be a picture of him in every home, and on the altars Mein Kampf and a sword.

7. Domination

The subtle effect of domination (often misplaced loyalty) results

in the circumscription of individuality.

This can be:

Parent — child (cultural)

Child — parent

Siblings

Married couples

Peers (cultural)

Employer — employee

Etc.

The limitation of circumscription is very painful to the person.

This often contributes to anxiety. Anxiety makes for inflexibility

and clinging to rigid belief systems which are considered

"RIGHT."

8. Interiorization, the Result of Combining Objective Sections A

and Subjective Section B

Two (2) primary factors emerge from a study of the socio-

economic and personal situation of the people of post WW I

Germany. These factors are (a) personal and (b) societal.

To understand their situation, these factors should be considered
in four ways:

    (1) Personally, for each citizen

    (2) As a group

    (3) As a person within the group and

    (4) As a group motivated by revengeful and re-
           empowerment aspirations

Between objective chaos and subjective rage, the collective mood

of hopelessness, struggle, and uncertainty prevailed. In the

context of history, the one man who was able, by determination

and charisma, to restore hope was the one who – due to his own

rage – was the most hopeless of all, Adolf Hitler.

References Cited In Part I

1. The Bible, King James Version, Genesis 4:8

2. The Nazis
   Time Life Books
   Robert E. Harzstein - 1980
   Pg. 23

3. To Destroy You Is No Loss - The Odyssey of a Cambodian Family
   by Joan D. Criddle
   Anchor Books, Doubleday
   N. Y.

4. In considering the barbaric pattern of conquest it should be noted that there is no civilized pattern of conquest since: (1) there is no civilization as yet; and (2) conquest would be inconceivable to a civilized person except as an historical concept.

   Throughout history the barbaric pattern of conquest has been that of castration of the men who are conquered, rape of the women who are conquered, and murder of the children who are conquered. It must be noted that these actions are the actions of total insanity. One may very well ask, "Where did this insanity come from?" If sex is evil, then participation in sex is also evil. If fear blocks the loving participation in sex (because of the assumption of evil) then the block may be overcome by insane actions, not sane (loving) actions. The actions of conquest are the freeing of the block to sexual action and proof of capacity despite the assumption of evil.

   There are economic motivations for conquest also, but these are incidental in terms of psychological motivation. The result of the barbaric pattern of conquest is the proof of sexual potency over sexual "evil" and a new genetic pattern in the area.

5. A Dance Between Flames
    By Anton Gill
    Carroll and Graf Publishers
    N. Y. – 1994
    Pg. 73

6. Hitler, A Study in Tyranny
    By Alan Bullock
    Bantam Books, Inc.
    N. Y., NY – 1961
    Pg. 17

7. The First World War
    By Martin Gilbert
    Henry Holt & Co.
    N. Y.
    Pgs. 516, 532

8. The World Book Encyclopedia
    233 N. Michigan
    Chicago, IL. 60601
    Pg. 340

9. Germany, 1866-1945
    By Gordon A. Craig
    Oxford University Press – 1980
    Pgs. 424, 425, 435

10. Politics and Diplomacy in Peacemaking: Containment and
    Counterrevolution at Versailles, 1918-1919
    By Arno J. Mayer
    N. Y. – 1967
    Chapters 15-17, 21, 22

11. Gods and Beasts, the Nazis and the Occult
    By Dusty Sklar
    Thomas Crowell Co. – 1977
    Pgs. 98, 110

12. Cosmic Consciousness by Dr. Richard M. Bucke, E.P. Dutton &
    Co., 1951

PART II

WWW

What Went Wrong in the

Life and Mind of Adolph Hitler

PART II

TABLE OF CONTENTS

General Statement of Approach to the Subject

When one visits bookstores, it is easy to see an average of one new book per month relating to Hitler. No person in the 20th century (now some 57 years after his suicide) has continued to hold not only interest, but fascination to the degree that Hitler has.

My work here is not toward a final analysis, but rather to summarize the psychological and historical forces involved with the aim of seeing how the holocaust must have naturally resulted from the combination of Germany 1918 through 1945 and the psyche and powers of Hitler.

Noting, especially, the psychological forces involved; indication will be made of how history may be changed if these forces are of sufficient magnitude.

CHAPTER 1

The Development of a Sado-Masochistic Personality

A sado-masochistic personality is one in which, due to physical and psychological trauma, sexual-affective forces become associated with the giving or receiving of pain.

The physical development of the child's nervous system is complete within age 4 (by the 5th birthday). (Reference 1)

Cellular development theory states that over a 7-year period, the body is completely regenerated. (All the cells are replaced over this time span.) (Reference ibid)

Hitler was beaten daily by his father from age 4 (Reference 2) to age 11 (Reference 3). This was (4-11) a total of 7 years.

If there is no possibility of physical escape (Reference 2, pg. 156), then someplace must be found to store the pain, energy, and desire-for-revenge which resulted from the beatings. This "storage place" was in every cell of the physical body. This RAGE, expressed as HATE, guided Hitler from age 11 on.

Hitler also faced the ultimate conflict of being _forced_ to love and honor his father who had caused him daily physical pain and psychological "put downs." (Reference 2, pgs. 156 and 157 and also Reference 9, pg. 240)

44

CHAPTER 2

The Jewish Grandfather Story, Myth, Assumption, Etc.

Research in the area of Hitler's family tree shows a continuing theme.

His father's father could possibly have been Jewish. (Reference 2, pgs. 147-156 and also Reference 4, pg. 10)

The psychological analysis given in Reference 2, pg. 148 is the best to be found. It shows that Hitler had no way of knowing, with any real certainty, who his grandfather was.

The Obliteration of Döllersheim

In May, 1938, Hitler ordered the residents of the Döllersheim area evacuated and the entire area used for mortar shell and tank practice. This completely destroyed the birthplace of his grandfather and grandmother.

CHAPTER 3

The Effect of His Father's Death at His Age 13

At the time of his father's death, at his age 13, Hitler made a decision that changed the world, and especially Europe, radically.

Due to his father's being dead, Hitler could not have his revenge against him personally for the daily beatings and psychological abuse which his father had given him.

There was always the possibility of his father being partly Jewish. So, the decision Hitler reached was that since he could not have revenge against his father personally, he would have revenge against ALL OF THEM. (Reference 1, pg. 7 and Reference 2, pg. 190)

CHAPTER 4

The Effect of His Mother's Death at His Age 18

General reading in the time span yields the impression that his mother, Klara, was the only person in life whom Hitler totally trusted. Gustl Kubizek was a companion for some years; but my impression is not that of trust.

Hitler returned to Urfahr from Vienna in late October, 1907 when advised by the doctor that his mother's health was failing. Her breast cancer had metastasized.

Both Reference 3, pg. 9 and Reference 4, pg. 29 indicate that Hitler's grief was *extremely* severe. One may well understand that his post-loss depression was also most severe.

CHAPTER 5

The Vienna Years and the Music of Wagner

Although he had lived in Vienna twice before, when he returned there in February, 1908, it was the beginning of a period of extreme poverty, difficultly, and depression for Hitler. (Reference 4, pgs. 32-54)

He was turned down three times by the Academy of Art. The first time he responded with rage and bitter denunciation. (Reference 4, pg. 33)

Much of the time until he left for Munich in May, 1913, he was living in what would now be called "homeless shelters."

These were times of acute depression. Hitler's mother had died (Reference 3 – The Path to Power, pg. 9) He had only one friend whom he could talk to (or perhaps talk at: Gustl Kubizek).

In these years, above all, Hitler needed a powerful force from _somewhere_ which could make his inner imaginary world correspond to some degree with his drab lower-class everyday existence as a laborer and small picture painter.

The music of Richard Wagner has always divided those who heard it into two (2) and _only_ two sets of responses: (1) they were awed, uplifted, and EMPOWERED, or (2) they had no use for it at all. There has never been a "gray area" of middle response to his music.

Hitler belonged totally to the first class, his need for empowerment was *extreme,* and in Wagner's music he found this need fully met.

The music of Wagner is different from that of any other great classical composer. The emotional effect produced is not dependent on the ensemble, the soloist, the duets, the melodic line, the choruses, the orchestration, or any other *musical* device. It depends totally on the *vibration.* This vibration *directly* affects the emotions of the listener.

This effect of *empowerment* explains the so-called "mystery" of Hitler's complete fascination with Wagner. How could a person so filled with hate and rage be so totally devoted to one composer, far above his "social class?"

After the years of daily beatings by his father, no one so desperately needed *empowerment* as did young Hitler. Finding this in Wagner's music meant that Hitler could achieve some degree of psychological stability while he discovered his oratorical ability and charisma. These are the two talents he used to (1) gain control of the NAZI party, and (2) become Chancellor of Germany, as head of the NAZI party (1-25-33).

It should also be noted that Hitler's contact with Wagner, through hearing his operas in Vienna, was soon after the death of his mother. Klara

Hitler was apparently the _only_ one Hitler completely trusted and her death left him in a state of extreme depression. (Reference 3, Volume I, pg. 29).

CHAPTER 6

Hitler's Army Service in WW I

Hitler retained his Austrian citizenship although he had moved to Munich. Austria requested that he report for induction into their army. On February 5, 1914, he was found too weak to serve.

One August 3, 1914, he volunteered for service in the Bavarian Army (a part of the German Army). On August 16, 1914, he was accepted. This was, at age 25, the first "regular job" he had ever had.

Much of his service was as a messenger between the front lines and regimental headquarters. He was promoted to Corporal. On August 4, 1918, he was awarded the Iron Cross, First Class. He barely escaped death many times. It appeared to him and others with him that he was protected by Providence. (Reference 4, pg. 67)

He was gassed in Belgium on August 14, 1918. He was hospitalized and later (November 1918) recovered from his temporary blindness.

After the Armistice of November 11, 1918, he was given the assignment of political agent by the army. His oratorical abilities flourished, and he became well known for his powers of speaking.

Germany, after the war (WW I), was in a state of political turmoil.

CHAPTER 7

Charisma

If we define "charisma" as the power or ability to change another person's belief system by verbal, empathic, and charming means, then the application of this definition is clearly evident in the case of Hitler.

The bond of those who suffer together is a very strong one; and the more severe the suffering, the greater is the empathic power generated.

This charismatic power, like all powers, may be used constructively or destructively. It can be used to convince people that evil is good, that expensive is cheap, that a non-existent charity is worthy of enormous contributions. (The example of the "con-man".)

Hitler's use of this power is well documented, particularly at the NAZI party rallies in Nuremberg and also by radio broadcasts and meetings.

CHAPTER 8

Propaganda and Charisma

NAZI propaganda, as delivered by Hitler, was notably monotonous

and boring. Despite this effect, it was greeted with enthusiasm and indeed a

shared fanaticism. The difference between the boring material and the

enthusiastic response can be described in one word: charisma. (See

Definition Section in Part I)

Dr. Joseph Goebbels, as chief of propaganda, devoted himself to

blaming the Jews exclusively for ALL that was wrong with Germany

between the wars. His approach was vitriolic hatred. This was the theme,

endlessly repeated, which unified the German belief system into a force

which Hitler could use to make the holocaust possible.

CHAPTER 9

Theories of the Source of Hitler's Charisma

At this point, we may consider three general theories or approaches to the question of "Where did Hitler's charismatic power come from?" These theories are:

I. Psychological

    In a group of children on the playground (or after school) usually one will be the instigator of new ideas. "Let's play so-and-so game, etc." This is evident from psychological studies of Hitler's childhood.

II. Empathic

    Biographical studies show that Hitler had experiences of unemployment and rejection by the Vienna Art Academy which gave him a sense of sympathy/empathy which could be used as a source of charisma when addressing a crowd.

III. Metaphysical

    The Spear of Destiny (Reference 4)

    This is a fascinating book which tells the story of the Spear of Longinus. At the time of the crucifixion, it became the repository of inconceivable power. Not power for good or evil,

54

just power. This power could be used either way. Hitler took

the destructive aspect of the power (Reference 3, pg 68).

Rudolph Steiner, author of many books on Christian mysticism

and the Holy Grail and founder of the Waldorf Schools, took

the constructive aspect of the power.

CHAPTER 10

The Beer Hall Putsch, Landsberg Prison (1923-1924) and The Writing of Mein Kampf

In 1923, Hitler and the NAZI party leadership became convinced that the ever accelerating inflation was a sufficiently disturbing factor to Germans in general that a Putsch (revolutionary movement) followed by a march on Berlin could succeed.

The plans that were made for this uprising were very incomplete. The date which was selected at the *Bürgerbräukeller* was November 8th. The police remained organized. Communications between various parts of the NAZIS broke down. There was a skirmish in the city (Munich), and a few were killed and wounded. Hitler's left arm was dislocated. He was taken into police custody at Uffing, a nearby Munich suburb. He was formally arraigned and sent to Landsberg Prison, 40 miles west of Munich. (Reference 4, Volume 1, Part 2, Chapter 6)

In Landsberg Prison

November 11, 1923 to December 20, 1924

While recovering from his very painful left shoulder dislocation and fracture, Hitler was, for some days, very dejected and refused to eat for two weeks.

Friends visited him for the purpose of uplift and encouragement. These included Anton Drexler, Knirsch, Frau Bechstein, and Helene Hanfstaengl. (Reference 4, Volume 1, Part 3, Chapter 7, pg. 191) They, individually or collectively, were able to rekindle his determination to (1) live and (2) resume political activity when he was released. His time alone in Cell #7 gave him a means of re-evaluation of the entire political situation. At this time, he thought of the highway (Autobahn) system; and also of the future famous car – the Volkswagen.

On February 26, 1924, his trial began. Hitler's oratorical powers had recovered, and he assumed the role of accuser, not that of defendant. His speeches produced profound effects on all those in the courtroom. He was sentenced to five years, less the six months already served.

Back in Landsberg, Hitler realized that the way to progress for the NAZI party was through winning elections (Ibid., pg. 205). Hitler converted most of the prison staff to his NAZI ideas (Ibid., pg. 207).

In the summer of 1924, Hitler worked intensely on *Mein Kampf*.

When asked if he had changed his methods of fighting Jewry, he repeated

that the harshest methods must be applied. (Ibid., pg 210)

On December 19, 1924, the Bavarian Supreme Court ordered Hitler's

immediate release.

When he returned to his home in Munich, he found his room filled

with flowers and laurel wreaths.

Although there were several severe emotional ups and downs in the

Putsch and Landsberg period, Hitler emerged in a state of much improved

confidence, understanding, and determination.

The Writing of *Mein Kampf*

Mein Kampf was written while Hitler was in Landsberg Prison from November 11, 1923 to December 20, 1924. He was not adverse to being worshiped. There should be a picture of *Der Führer*, and on the altar *Mein Kampf*, and a sword. In this book, Hitler clearly described his plan – genocide – for the Jews. (Reference 10, pg. 148)

The book is also an autobiography – not always accurate. It is also a statement of political philosophy: racism, nationalism, and judeophobia.

Reference 10, pgs. 151 and 152 lists 25 statements of ANTI-Jewish propaganda.

It is filled with countless repetitions of self-justification and projected blame.

CHAPTER 11

The Use of Forces Available Through Time

Hitler was well aware of his three primary powers: (1) charisma, (2) oratory, and (3) determination.

Following release from Landsberg Prison, Hitler set out (1) to rebuild the NAZI party and (2) through it, to gain control of Germany *legally*. The worldwide depression of 1929 helped the NAZI cause.

With the taking of control by Hitler of the NAZI party on July 29, 1921, the *revenge of the child* ever-increasingly became the *revenge of the children*. From 1926 onward, the famous Nuremberg NAZI Party Rallies added: (1) Spectacle, (2) Music, and (3) Uniforms to the process of building, in the minds and hearts of the German people, the firm idea of a one-party government, run by an absolute dictator, Hitler. Twelve years of effort was victorious on January 30, 1933, when Hitler became Chancellor.

The traditional *Three Graces* = Faith, Hope, and Charity (Love) were increasingly replaced by the NAZI version: (Reference 3, Volume 1, pg. 230)

FAITH

HOPE

HATRED

A popular NAZI song was "The Hymn of Hate."

Dr. Joseph Goebbels, chief of the NAZI propaganda department, continued endlessly with his focus of blame and projection: "It was the *JEWS* who were responsible for <u>all</u> the ills and problems of Germany."

Over time, the propaganda removed any sense of denial in the minds of the German masses; and brought them into a state of ever-greater recognition of their feelings of hatred and the desire to destroy.

The approval of a father, or of an approving *father image* (such as a chief-of-state) was certainly one of the greatest and deepest needs of the mass of formerly abused children. This approval opened the door to the *action* of revenge.

Through the effect of NAZI propaganda on the minds of Germans, the Jews became SYMBOLS of all that was wrong in Germany. Accordingly, the size of the SYMBOL was only limited by imagination. (Reference 2, pgs. 190 and 191)

So it was that one rage (Hitler's) expressed through many rages, came to destroy:

1. Freedom

2. Business

3. Culture and

4.   Life itself

In this way, Hitler was able to *act out* his desire for revenge against:

1.   His father (who had died on January 3,

1903)

2.   The Jews, and

3.   The World (World War II)

CHAPTER 12

The Army Bomb Plot

From November 1943 onward, there was ever-increasing army discontent with the way the war was going; also with Hitler's inflexible position regarding tactics and strategy. (Reference 3, Volume II, pgs 883 – 931)

Realizing Hitler's vacillation and complete determination to "do things his way", many top field marshals and generals concluded that eliminating Hitler was the only way to bring the war to a successful or even reasonable conclusion.

Several attempts were planned but not completed due to circumstantial factors. When the Allies struck on June 6, 1944 with "D-Day" and the Normandy Invasion, the Germans were faced with three wars at once:

1. The West

2. Russia – the Stalingrad fiasco, and

3. the Jews

Better aircraft design had given the Allies superiority in the air; and resources exhaustion was an ever-greater possibility.

On July 21, 1944, a bomb exploded at a high-level military conference; again Hitler survived by circumstances.

Hitler felt that his bond of trust had been betrayed, and the violence of his reaction startled both the NAZIS and Germans in general. He had the leading conspirators impaled on meat hooks and then strangled by the piano wire of the Gestapo. Friends of relatives of friends of relatives were arrested, tortured, and executed. Almost 5,000 persons died.

In January 1945, the last effort on the part of Germany to win WW II, the "Battle of the Bulge" was won instead by the Allied forces. Germany was progressively invaded from east and west.

Many accounts of the death of Hitler have been written and published. Perhaps the best one at capturing the actual feeling of the events of April 30, 1945 in the air raid bunker in Berlin is Reference 3, Chapter 31, pgs. 998 - 1005.

Hitler's last acts of revenge were against his dog, Blondi, who like his mistress/bride of one day, Eva Braun, was given or took poison; and against himself.

References Cited In Part II

1. Hitler, The Path to Power
   By Charles B. Flood
   Houghton Mifflin Co., 1989

   Pg. 7   Revenge, search for an enemy to punish. Age 11
   Pg. 9   Grief at his mother's death. Age 18
   Pg. 62   1919 "All the fault of the Jews"
   Pg. 74   Hitler joined the Nazi party – October 1919
   Pg. 78   Oratorical power
   Pg. 82   Avenge Versailles
   Pg. 204   Hitler controls Nazi party – July 29, 1921
   Pg. 451   1 trillion marcs = $1.00
   Pg. 566   4.6 trillion marcs = $1.00 (1923)
   Pg. 600   Chancellor – January 30, 1933

2. "For Your Own Good"
   By Dr. Alice Miller
   Farrar-Straus-Giroux – 1983

   Pages 5 through 7
   Rage storage, Pg. 146

3. Adolph Hitler
   By John Toland
   Two Volumes – Doubleday

4. The Spear of Destiny
   By Trevor Ravenscroft
   Ref re Rudolph Steiner
   Published by Samuel Weiser
   York Beach, Maine

5. Hitler – A Study in Tyranny
   By Alan Bullock

6. The Anatomy of Human Destructiveness
   By Erich Fromm
   Holt, Reinhart, & Winston – 1973

7. Mein Kampf
   By Adolph Hitler
   Translated by Ralph Manheim
   Boston, 1943

   Hitler was lower middle class.
   He had a great educational urge.

Pg. XII	Lack of concern for the objective world.
Pg. XIII	RAGE
Pg. XV	"White-hot hatred" – Claim to supreme leadership
Pg. XIX	The book may well be called a kind of satanic Bible
	Men not equal was the purpose of the book
Pg. XX	Hitler always sees blood
Ch. I	Invoking FATE
Pg. 6	"great heroic struggle" became "my greatest inner experience"
	Father a "domineering nature"
Pg. 9	Conflict with his father re: his becoming a civil servant
Pg. 10	Anti-Semitic
Pg. 13	"I became a fanatical German Nationalist."
Pg. 14	"To learn history is to see and find the forces which cause .... historical events.
Pg. 15	"budding nationalistic fanatic"
Pg. 16	"destroy Austria."

8. Soul Murder: Persecution in the Family
   By Morton Schatzman
   Random House, NY – 1973

   This is the same as The Dark Teaching referred to in Dr. Alice
   Miller's book "For Your Own Good"

   Fr. Daniel Schreber. He followed totalitarian methods on his own two
   sons. One was a suicide. The other spent most of his life in mental
   institutions.

9. Character Analysis
   By Wilhelm Reich
   Farrar, Straus, and Giroux
   New York

10. The History of an Obsession
    By Klaus Fischer
    Continuum Publishing Co.
    New York

PART III

WWW

What Went Wrong as a

Result of the Combination

of Parts I and II

PART III

TABLE OF CONTENTS

CHAPTER 1

Introduction

The total rage and denial of the generation which became the NAZIS may be compared to an explosive.

The ignition may be compared to Hitler's rage and charisma combined with the propaganda of Dr. Joseph Goebbels.

The explosion was the Holocaust.

CHAPTER 2

General Treatment of Children in the Raising of the Generation That Became the NAZIS

"Soul Murder, Persecution in the Family" by Morton Schatzman (Reference 1) gives a general idea, especially in the Methods Section, of what was done to this generation by their parents. This is the generation that became the NAZIS. It is a parallel book, in English, to the "Schwarze Pädagogik" (The Black Teaching) which is available only in German. In the latter part of the 1800's, a Dr. Schreber wrote a series of books on child-rearing. Some went through forty (40) printings and were considered a primary guide to correct and effective child-raising in Germany. (Reference 1)

Understanding this will enable a reader to grasp, to some degree, the potential of rage and hatred that was present in the generation that became the NAZIS.

CHAPTER 3

The Goal of Abuse

The goal of abuse was to produce a child who was:

1. Docile

2. Attentive

3. Obeyed instantly

4. Loved the abuser (parent)

The psychological conflict caused by being forced to love someone who was a constant source of pain and invasion makes a base for the personality which is *extremely* unstable. One-to-one bonding is not possible. Socialization is minimal. A generation raised in abuse will have no consideration of another person's rights or possessions. Group bonding will be for purposes of destruction.

A person raised in an abusive setting will obey orders without any thought whatsoever as to the effect or result of these orders. If the person giving the orders is himself enraged, then there is no limit to the amount of destruction which will be created.

CHAPTER 4

Propaganda as Blame

The NAZIS used propaganda as a system for changing how the average citizen perceived reality. This system involved five elements:

1. Radio

2. Movies

3. Speeches at gatherings

4. Book sales "Mein Kampf"

5. Party rallies (the most famous being at Nurenberg)

All of these elements were directed toward showing that it was the JEWS who were responsible, and so to blame, for ALL the national problems:

UNEMPLOYMENT

INFLATION

SOCIAL UNREST

THE WEAK WEIMAR GOVERNMENT

THE LOSS OF THE WAR (1914 – 1918)

THE TREATY OF VERSAILLES

ETC., ETC.

And accordingly should suffer and be totally destroyed.

73

CHAPTER 5

General Genocide

People often think of "The Holocaust" only as the insult, pain, and mass death which happened at the concentration camps; but the NAZI application of anti-semitism-as-blame was far more general than a variety of ways of dying.

Every aspect of life, and indeed of existence itself, was to be completely removed:

Social

Cultural

Political

Economic

Religious

Educational

Professional

Etc., etc.

CHAPTER 6

The Invasion Principle

Child abuse is INVASION; an invasion of the sanctity, the space, the psyche and/or the body of the child.

The burglar, thief, con-man, rapist is an INVADER. The "criminal mind" is formed BY invasion, and reacts WITH invasion. This effect, plus lack of instruction in ethical principles, makes for domestic crime in peacetime.

The same effect — aided by Hitler's charisma — and organized by the NAZI party — became the invasive force in WW II. This force conquered Europe and came perilously close to conquering our planet.

CHAPTER 7

RAGE — Transformation by Pain

Rage is not national. It can be inventive. It is pure destructive force.

It is the ultimate response to burdens which the individual is unable to bear.

In the process of assuming control of the conscious mind, it made the

Holocaust possible.

CHAPTER 8

RAGE — The Pack Spirit

The blocking of the forward force of life itself (evolution) results in the appearance of a most awesome power. This power represents the determination of the force of life to go through the block. This power of - itself is blind and meaningless. Destruction of any convenient target is inevitable once this power is unleashed. (Reference Part I)

This power is against life in whatever form the target may be. The reason for this is that the target has come to mean the blockage itself.

Propaganda and training of the youth TOWARD prejudice can make any group a suitable target in any country.

An example of this in the animal kingdom is a pack (group) of tame dogs who become wild in the presence of a group of rabbits. In this example, the motivation is hunger.

In the human situation, the motivation is revenge; whether individual (burglary, rape, and murder); or group "organized crime" (the mafia, drugs, prostitution) or national ("weapons of mass destruction") biological, neurological, or atomic — the purpose is the same, DESTRUCTION of the targeted individual or group.

77

Animals lack the utilization of technology and "linear (left brain) thinking". Humans, using these additional powers, are quite capable at present (A.D. 2002) of extinguishing life from an entire planet, the earth for example.

In Hitlerian times, an example of the "pack spirit" is the groups of NAZI military forces, well equipped with knives, swords, automatic weapons, and explosives who set out and attacked Polish villages at the start of the war (~ 1939). The villages and their inhabitants ceased to exist. It is said that "no group in history could ever equal the ferocity of these roving bands."

All revengeful actions, horrors, were carried out, as exactly as possible, as equals to what the child, who later became the NAZI, received when *they* were a child. They were carried out against *many* because of the amount of rage in each child, later a NAZI.

CHAPTER 9

Two Horrors

Horrors:

1) That education, viz, PhD's from German Universities, did not yield any sense of mercy or compassion.

1A) Intellect without ethical understanding is cold and unfeeling.

2) Variety of punishment given at the Concentration Camps: viz, beating, burning, rape, "medical experiments", starvation, etc., etc.

2A) Those empowered by the NAZI government to carry out "The final solution to the Jewish Question" were given the power of choice as to their actions.

What determined this choice?

I. The type of abuse which they had received, specifically "acted out" in psychological terms.

II. RAGE

CHAPTER 10

Two Desires

The survivors have two notable desires: (1) to be remembered, and (2) to prevent further Holocausts.

1) History and the current literature on the subject will accomplish the desire to be remembered.

2) Hopefully this book will be of help in prevention.

CHAPTER 11

Types of Re-Empowerment

Choice of type of death = means = ultimate power = ultimate destructive re-empowerment. This was the function of the camps. They felt as though they had been to hell and so duplicated hell as a means of revenge.

The NAZIS, the camps, and the Holocaust were accordingly the outward mechanism of re-empowerment. This re-empowerment was a necessary revengeful response to the disempowerment suffered by the generation which became the NAZIS. **This disempowerment was caused by severe child abuse activated in the post WW I milieu of confusion, inflation, and unemployment — all guided by Hitler's own desire for revenge and directed through the power of his charisma and oratorical skill.**

CHAPTER 12

Destructive Re-Empowerment

Power is taken from the child by the process of abuse.

Re-empowerment may be of two (2) types:

      (1)   Healing

              By various kinds of psychotherapy.

      (2)   Revenge

              The projection of destructive energy; outward as crime or inward as illness.

The choice of the type of re-empowerment depends on (A) the awareness of society of the damage done to the child and (B) the willingness of society to heal the child.

Both factors in Germany between the wars, were essentially and effectively ZERO.

Accordingly, the potential for destructive re-empowerment was very great.

CHAPTER 13

The Formalization of the Decision for Genocide
"The Final Solution to the Jewish Question"

Prior to the full implementation of the Holocaust, indeed with the NAZI voted take-over of the German government (Hitler's Chancellership on January 30, 1933) there had been many violent state-supported anti-Jewish actions. These were only indications of what was to come.

The Wannsee Conference

This conference, held on January 20, 1942, served to unify the entire NAZI government in the matter of a policy of genocide: death for all the Jews in Europe. Since Goebbels' propaganda had convinced the mass of Germans that the Jews *were to blame for all* the difficulties encountered since November 11, 1918, this meant that the Jews should be *punished* as well as destroyed.

CHAPTER 14

The Organization of Genocide

The following divisions of the NAZI government were involved:

The Gestapo

Race and Settlement Main Office

Central Government

Security Police — RIGA

Ministry of the Interior

Office of the Governor-General

Office of the Four-Year Plan

Ministry of Justice

The Foreign Office

The Reich's Chancellery

The NAZI Party Chancellery

The Ministry of the Occupied Eastern Territories

The Chief Reich Administration Offices

The "SS" (Schützstaffel)

Central Agency for Jewish Emigration

(Reference 1, pg. 352)

CHAPTER 15

Control

The "Final Solution" also gave the ones who *operated* the camps

TOTAL CONTROL of the inmates. This is the final state of tyranny. It

means that ALL aspects of the inmate's life:

> Food
>
> Water
>
> Clothing
>
> Air:
>
>> Poisoning of air
>>
>> Air pressure
>
> Sex
>
> Elimination
>
> Activities:
>
>> Often to amuse the operators
>
> Degree of pain
>
> Temperature
>
> Type of death
>
> Etc.

were totally controlled by the operators.

Control reversal can serve as psychological healing. The NAZIS could give death for the taking (distortion) of their lives by those who had abused *them*.

Once reversal of control was established, there was no limit to the amount and variety of mis-use of the power.

The abusees (the NAZI generation) were TOTALLY controlled by those who abused them in their childhood.

Total control of one individual by another is against the force of evolution itself which is aimed toward individualization of expression of idea in form and action.

Individual desires for some type of revengeful action were fulfilled by the range of types of pain and death provided at the concentration camps.

Anything beyond the historically based types of death-causing methods was provided by RAGE itself, the most destructive type of total insanity.

The power of death-over-life is the ultimate control in moments of revenge by the individual. This same power is the ultimate control by society in *its* moments of revenge.

CHAPTER 16

The Power of Death-Over-Life

As we have seen in Part I, Section B, the abused child, coming into life, seeking love, finds instead the immediate threat of death, expressed as hate, pain, invasion, and demoralization.

The ultimate threat is the threat of death. This threat was expressed to the child in the generation which became the NAZIS in a variety of ways according to the type of abuse received: physical, sexual, verbal, emotional, etc.

In the process of survival in spite of the abuse, the power of denial was used by each child. Using this power means that the energy of the experience of the abuse was transferred to the subconscious mind. From the subconscious mind, the energy was released in a variety of actions. These actions corresponded to a perfect balancing reaction to the actions of the abuse, as closely as could be arranged to achieve a complete, though displaced, revenge. These actions, in the form of words, pictures, and memories are still horrifying to the world over 50 years later. They represent a variety of ways of dying as forms of amusement (revenge).

The NAZI party was organized to (1) bring economic and political stability to post WW I Germany and (2) to use the power of this stability to achieve revenge by enslavement, genocide, and war.

CHAPTER 17

The Generalization of Death

To produce death, a severe stress must be placed on the body or mind or nervous system. Beheading would work, but so would bleeding to death. Hanging would work, but so also would strangulation, ETC., ETC., ad infinitum.

CHAPTER 18

The Methodology of Murder

Death by excess of stress:

1) Physical:

    Heat

    Cold

    No food

    No water

    Air pressure

    Poison

    Poison Gas

    Disease

    Exhaustion

    Temperature

    Etc.

2) Neurological:

    An over stimulated nervous system

90

3)   Psychological:

    Interrupted sleep —

       This was called "Going to the

       Theater" when it resulted in

       hallucinations.

CHAPTER 19

Symbol and Actuality

At the time of the establishment of the NAZI regime in post WW I Germany, the state, in the role of the *approving* father figure (Adolph Hitler), gave to the abused generation, the NAZIS, the power of exacting their revenge. This was a revenge both symbolic and actual, against a group, the Jews, who were innocent, local, and available.

The actions of this revenge constituted the destructive re-empowerment of the abused generation which had joined the NAZI party with so much hope for some improvement in their desperate condition (See Part I).

Based on his own desire for revenge against his father and the power of his charisma, Hitler replaced FAITH, HOPE, and CHARITY (LOVE) with:

FAITH

HOPE

and HATE

Under the NAZI regime, great improvements were made in industry, commerce, highways, employment, and economic stability. Opposing groups were eliminated (usually by killing them).

But the need for blame and so for revenge remained.

SINGLE

The Jewish grandfather myth (?). *Suspicion was enough.* Hitler's father was, therefore, a *symbol.* Therefore, eliminate *ALL* to eliminate his father. He could not kill his father as his father had already died. ALL, therefore, served as a symbol of *one* (his father).

GROUP

Actions done to relieve incandescent stress on the part of the most abused ones (the 100,000 to 500,000 volunteers who were the actual operators of the camps).

Symbolic action was taken psychologically, *actual* action was taken physically — as none could take revenge directly on their parents, siblings, peers, teachers, etc. for what had been done *to them.*

Rage was the blocked evolutionary power, the force-of-life of an entire generation — all those who participated obeyed the FIAT, "KILL THE JEWS."

If Germany had won the war (WW II), this same force could have destroyed the world in mindless fury.

CHAPTER 20

The Specificity of Revenge

As information on the range and variety of atrocities committed became available to the world community, largely since 1945, a sense of horrified fascination and wonder arose due to the variety and type of punishment which was inflicted. (Reference to Part I, Types of Child Abuse)

An explanation of this may be found in the various types of child abuse which was inflicted on children in Germany; specifically on the generation which became the NAZIS.

Every personality seeks balance and peace. If the balance and peace is attained by destructive group re-empowerment, then the consequence of a variety of horrors will follow.

If the child who became the NAZI was beaten by his parents, peers, or teachers, then he *did* the beating or *watched* the beating taking place.

If he was starved, then he *set up* the conditions for the starvation of the prisoners or *watched* the starvation happen.

If he was made to work extremely long and hard, then he could work in the infamous "Arbeit zur Tod," work-to-death section. Etc., etc.,

It should be noted that the entire variety of horrors was directed toward obtaining amusement and satisfaction (revenge) by imposing the ultimate control of a variety of types of death on the prisoners. This control could be obtained either directly (by participating) or symbolically (by watching and listening to the screams).

CHAPTER 21

Reason for the Variety of Horrors

All of the horrors were PLAYING WITH THE FORCE-OF-LIFE.

The abused child has had his/her force-of-life interrupted, stopped, stymied by pain, assault, INVASION, and interruption. This is an extremely serious matter to the child.

To be able to *PLAY* with another person's force-of-life on a life-or-death basis; from a control standpoint; was revenge for the (now-adult-age) child.

97

CHAPTER 22

The Confluence of Factors to Produce a Holocaust

The Historic Combination of :

1) Someone to blame, a "them"

2) These persons must be:

   A. Local

   B. Innocent

   C. Available

3) Objective hopelessness throughout society

4) A means of contact — RADIO, MOVIES, MEETINGS

5) Charisma — EMPATHY

6) Rallies at Nurenburg

7) A book, "MEIN KAMPF" which focuses the blame

8) Action — through a governmental organization and policy — to transfer *by projection* the pain of child abuse to those who are "to blame."

9) Completion by reversing the control.

CHAPTER 23

Summary

The reservoir of rage within Hitler combined with the *belief/supposed possibility* that his grandfather *might have been* Jewish produced a focus of hate which was boundless.

The next part of the combination was the repressed rage of the German people at *their own* child abuse which they had received.

The third part of the combination was the ceaseless radio propaganda of Dr. Joseph Gobbels. This propaganda changed the *belief* of the German people to one in which the only reduction of stress possible was through Jewish genocide.

The result of this combination was the Holocaust.

References Cited In Part III

1. The History of an Obsession
   By Klaus Fischer
   Continuum Publishing Co.,
   N. Y.

PART IV

WWW

What We Want

A World Without Violence,

Crime, And War

PART IV

TABLE OF CONTENTS

God-in-Action

Have you ever beheld---

God-in-action

Creating, all-rejoicing

a rose

A galaxy

A sunset --- cloud by cloud

Or entering a room, manifested

as a little child?

— from the Songs of Chandra Lal

103

CHAPTER 1

Complex and Simplex

COMPLEX

Complex is that the world-wide problems related to crime, violence, drugs, and WAR are very complex and inter-related.

SIMPLEX

Simplex is that they can be effectively removed by raising one (1) generation of UN-abused children.

104

CHAPTER 2

General Comment

Unless each generation is farther from the Chain of Darkness (child abuse), the only progress made by humanity is toward greater, more efficient destruction.

The colossal and ever-growing, potential of each generation for both building and destroying *must* be directed toward peace and the positive virtues of art, music, nature, and greater understanding.

This potential exists in the child, and humanity can only receive the blessing of the constructive use of this potential from an *unabused* child.

The emotions of the abused child are far too rapidly changing and uncontrollable to permit time ... and energy to be used for the finishing of constructive projects. Meanwhile, the desire for revenge continues, in a world of miniaturization and atomic power.

There are no generations which the world can help except those we see now as parents and children.

Human behavior is variable as to type of activity and intensity, but not accidental. It has definite purposes, whether constructive or destructive. It also has motivation, a goal. This is based on history.

The fundamental relationship of forces:

IF DIRECTED OUTWARD:

<u>CRIME AND VIOLENCE</u>

IF DIRECTED INWARD:

<u>ILLNESS AND LACK OF</u>

<u>ACCOMPLISHMENT</u>

CHAPTER 3

What Is So Precious As The Child?

1. All future evolutionary possibilities are contained in each generation.

2. Ever – new expression of all talents AND future inventions upon which all progress depends is also there.

3. Each one contributes to the whole.

4. Love given by each is to the whole.

5. There is no human future without the child.

6. All talents are given TO BE USED by society. If one talent or invention is not used, then society is shorted.

7. Positive capacity/potential becomes negative destructive potential by abuse and so <u>COSTS</u> society VERSUS contribution *to* society.

8. Each new generation brings with it, the total potential of our evolution on the planet to date. The wonders it can discover and bring forth are beyond imagining. But, none of this can happen unless the life of each child is treasured.

SUBJECTIVE I

Understand that all hope for the future of our world depends on action taken to help each generation become greatly LESS ABUSED. Only in this way can the chain-of-darkness be broken.

SUBJECTIVE II

Understand that in constructive work, action follows thought. Understand that in destructive work, thought follows action.

OBJECTIVE I

Take all the actions noted above, here in Part IV, to decrease the amount of child abuse.

OBJECTIVE II

Continue in the needed actions until a non-abused generation is produced. This generation will have non-abused children and the world will become non-violent.

CHAPTER 4

The Force Of Evolution

Irrespective of the traditional view of Instantaneous Creation (8:05 a.m., Saturday, October 10, 7007 B.C. or the evolutionary view of 360 million years of cosmic divine evolution), the fact remains that each successive generation has with it and indeed brings with it an awesome force for interest, exploration, and the living of life itself.

Anyone who presents an obstacle or deterrent to the creative expression of this force does so at their greatest peril and peril for the world.

The force is the desire to live in order to (1) give love and (2) be loved.

All abuse is the expression of fear which is the opposite of love and is therefore directed against the force-of-life which comes with each successive generation.

The necessarily constructive energy of the entire NAZI generation (*to start*) was blocked by the shock and pain of abuse and re-directed – to become one of the most TOTALLY DESTRUCTIVE forces in all of human history.

CHAPTER 5

The Potential Of Forgiveness

The human spirit is very durable and one should not deny the constructive potential of forgiveness.

E.g., the BI-PARTISAN government in South Africa. The lady TV announcer with tears, "I wondered and doubted that I would ever see this day — when black forgives white."

CHAPTER 6

Child Raising

Having a child should, of all experiences, make all persons aware of the Preciousness and Dignity of Life.

One should not have children unless there is love in the heart for each child.

Psychological abuses of childhood can – and do – last through a lifetime. The child searching for the love needed from BOTH parents is the primary psychological force in life.

CHAPTER 7

The Chain-Of-Darkness Is Hard To Break

The factors:

      I.   Past abuse (in all) as irritation in the NOW

      II.   Stress level/energy level in the NOW

      III.   Loss of emotional physical control in the NOW

The Present Response of Society is that "Child Abuse is an Effect."

Actually, Child Abuse is a CAUSE. Not only a cause, but an endlessly re-circulating totally destructive cause.

CHAPTER 8

Destiny

I. 80% of those incarcerated have child abuse in their history; stealing, and prostitution are for drugs.

II. Children take drugs because:

1) lack of information regarding the danger

2) peer pressure

3) lack of love from parents, a natural "HIGH" versus an artificial "high" from neuro chemistry

Individual decision

For a given person (parent) in a given instant, the question is which of two things will triumph and determine the immediate action taken.

These are:

1) The sweetness and innocence of the child or

2) Anger based on the parent's *own* abuse. (The chain-of-darkness)

CHAPTER 9

Saving The World One Child At A Time

"Ultimate Heroism"

Not outward, but inward control and peace is needed.

It is so simple:

DO NOT STRIKE!

The child is adapting the best he/she can at the moment, and is depending on a peaceful and supportive response by the "GROWN-UP" PERSON/PARENT.

This dependence is TOTAL.

CHAPTER 10

Parental Attitudes Needed

I.   Be aware of tiredness

II.   Avoid overwhelmed feeling

III.   Accept differences of life style

IV.   Keep flexible

V.   Avoid separation

VI.   Avoid projection

VII.   WITNESS anger, don't act on it

VIII. Avoid recycles

IX.   Reference "Care of the Soul" by Thomas Moore

Parents who abuse cut off their own source of great amounts of love from their children.

Both child and parent have come to earth *to find love*.

CHAPTER 11

The Awesome Power Of Love

Consider that all psychological powers are used to defend the self against trauma, and that 6 million lives could have been saved by HUGS each day for ADOLF HITLER.

Enormous amounts of time and energy are spent in child raising. All this is wasted unless there is kindness and support. Only with bonding which gives a foundation to the personality is there a basis from which the child can successfully operate.

Accept patience from the evolutionary force itself.

CHAPTER 12

Guarding The Growing Treasure

A primary and most essential part of making the change in society from abused to un-abused is to provide child-care for the new generation of the un-abused.

The care-takers must be BY DEFINITION un-abused themselves.

The un-abused child-care field will be ever growing as the final victory proceeds.

CHAPTER 13

What Is Left After The Abuse

All that is available to each person after their abuse is the undamaged abilities, memories, etc. which are still available; these are the capacities not destroyed by the various types of pain and insult which they have received.

Making use of what is left means that each person must set up habits to survive and make progress. Using these habits often makes great difficulties for the person because the habit; which is all they have left to use; does not relate well (or at all) to their current situation.

All of this increases the total stress of society. Accordingly, each abuse not done reduces the total stress of society and helps prevent accidents, etc.

After abuse, all that remains is a *part* of the talent, ability and strength of the original personality.

Years of therapy can help, but there is no way to tell what gifts never arrive in society. Another Mozart, Da Vinci, or Einstein?

After abuse, all that remains of the original personality structure is fragments and remnants and the desire to gain revenge.

Abuse distorts the belief structure of the child. So, limiting the child's possibility of action.

Abuse results in an incomplete person. A part of the energetic capacity of the person is locked interminably in an emotional conflict. Some part of the person, some talent, interest, or inventiveness is forever lost to the world.

Abuse destroys the ability to have a definite sequence and FOCUS of emotions. This is needed for the progress in all areas. Destruction vs construction (hard to progress).

CHAPTER 14

Legislation

A Federal law is needed which will greatly increase Child Protective
Services.

The action of this law must extend to:

State

County

City

Township

District

Precinct

Block

It is well known that delay in Congress in the human rights area is
interminable.

Accordingly, "Grass Roots" action is urgently and immediately
needed.

The Federal law should set age 18 as the minimum child-bearing age.
Education regarding birth-control (actually pregnancy control) is absolutely
essential. (Reference 11)

Dog licenses are required for dog ownership. The right to bear children is considered "sacred;" how can it be *sacred* if it is not *kind*?

CHAPTER 15

Diagnosis To Healing

Tattoos and body piercing

Abuse is the invasion/destruction of individuality and individual
expression. Tattooing is the symbolic healing of this attack. By producing a body
bearing unique designs, the psyche is able to regain an increased sense of the
sacred individuality.

Body piercing is most often seen in those parts of the body related to
sexual activity: penis, clitoris, labia minora, nipples, also speech and the
organs of sensory input: eyebrows, lips, nose, and ears.

These are all the areas of former physical and/or verbal abuse. Silver
is noted for its purity. The injured psyche desperately needs purity and
healing where pain and invasion were received, saying to the world, "I was
hurt *HERE!*" NOTE: Not all tattooing comes from abuse. Some is a "lark"
or misjudgment.

Psychological support in the home and ethics courses (from kindergarten on up) are training systems which *can prevent crime.*

Prevention cost versus crime cost is not currently understood. Prevention cost is very small compared to:

1)   Training and equipping police

2)   Apprehension

3)   Judicial process:

     a.   Legal training

     b.   Court building (construction)

     c.   Court operation

4)   Incarceration and detention

5)   Prison construction

6)   Prison operation

7)   Probation and parole

CHAPTER 16

Ways Of Prevention

How to prevent future Holocausts:

I.   Eliminate child abuse world wide

We have seen the same forces acting in the former Yugoslavia, Zaire, Cambodia, Iran, and in the USA. The example being the (inadvertent) arming of the children and the resultant school shootings.

II.   Prevent the roots of violence from growing

A.   Stop projecting parental athletic non-accomplishment onto children. Let the children live their own lives. Reference 10

B.   Water birth for peaceful entry into this world — Lamaze. (Reference 3)

C.   *Required* classes in parenting and bonding with your child.

People are not *naturally* criminals. They *become* criminals because of what has happened to them. Abuse is an *emotional training process* which *produces* criminals.

CHAPTER 17

Ways Of Protecting Society

Without the unabused child, there will be no *existence* of society.

Consider the present downward spiral:

    I.   Drugs

    II.   Violence

    III.   "Babies having babies"

The problem is <u>PRIORITY</u> which yield more prisons, vast danger, and suffering.

In former times of family cohesion and stability, there was little divorce and more control over reproduction; (less unplanned pregnancy), *but not now.*

So — other ways must be found: intensive education in the areas of sexually transmitted diseases (STDs) and birth control (actually pregnancy control).

CHAPTER 18

Crime Prevention

I. The elimination/great decrease in birth trauma

The system still so often used of holding the newborn by the ankles in

bright light and spanking provides *enormous shock* to the nervous

system.

The Lamaze water birth system greatly decreases the amount of birth

trauma. (Reference 3)

II. Without child abuse, life can proceed peacefully. Challenges can be

in the area of learning rather than in the area of physical/emotional

survival.

III. Without feelings of danger, there is no need for revenge reactions.

CHAPTER 19

Ways Of Preventing School Shootings

Until the Freedom Generation (the unabused generation) arrives, a primary way of improving the entire situation of child-society interaction is to:

LISTEN TO THE CHILD

If they speak of hating others,

1)   TAKE IT TOTALLY SERIOUSLY

2)   DO THERAPY IMMEDIATELY

3)   SEPARATE GUNS AND CHILDREN

Many lives can be saved in this way, including that of the child.

CHAPTER 20

Lessons Learned Or To Be Learned

The entire Holocaust experience in terms of such concepts as racial memory (not used in the NAZI sense of "racial") or societal attitudes is a lesson in understanding the evolutionary power or force-of-life which arrives with each generation. This awesome force, if blocked or distorted, can turn and destroy whole societies.

The fact that child abuse and exploitation continues in our society and to greater or lesser extent throughout our world (March 2002) is evidence that the lesson of respect for the previousness and dignity of life indeed HAS NOT been learned.

It is the non-learning that makes the great danger to society, the great danger to "civilization" itself.

CHAPTER 21

How To Break The Cycle

I. Therapy for child by law.

II. Therapy for abuser by law.

III. Education regarding the destructive effects of child abuse. Courses included in all grade levels by law.

IV. Great increase in Child Protective Services versus the *fresh* blood and *fresh* scars now required.

CHAPTER 22

Current Costs Of Crime

The cost of child abuse is $56 billion per year. (Reference 10)

1) Is this approach /expense necessary?

2) Could there be a better approach?

     a)   Less expensive?

     b)   More productive of a better world?

THINK!　　ACT!

CHAPTER 23

What To Do In Present Time

Note parallels:

Inflation

Quest for meaning

Satanic worship by children

Any group will serve as victims

USA has maximum violence

I. Increase water birth to cancel three stages of:

    a. Birth trauma

    b. Abuse

    c. Circumstance

II. Eliminate child abuse

III. Eliminate drug use by loving the children

IV. Educate to understand the need for love. This is not Valentines.

V. Eliminate prejudice by education.

VI. Build self-esteem versus any need for power and revenge.

CHAPTER 24

Systems Of Belief And Their Relation To Reality

A belief about some object, person, custom, or relationship is actually only another thought. However, if it is taught by an *authority figure* and *ACCEPTED* as *TRUE*, it gains the power to *control action* in the *individual* and/or *collective* psyche.

If a belief is a *projection* of *HATE* and *FEAR*, then this belief has *collectively*, the power to destroy the lives and works of many people.

The fact that the belief is *FALSE* does not make any difference. The destructive effect is the *same*.

So, the problem of creating a world free of war, hate, and destruction is the problem of changing belief systems so that they correspond to reality. Reality is the universal expression of love.

CHAPTER 25

The Immediate Destiny Of Mankind

Hate, fear, and violence are present in our world.

Atomic and biological weaponry, the result of fear, are also in our world.

All of this is because of the need for *revenge*.

This work has presented a peaceful, loving way of eliminating the motive of revenge by eliminating child abuse.

This can only be done by *applying* the systems noted above in Part IV. Many individual choices are involved. On these choices depend the group choices; on the group choices depend the representative choice of government.

Let us save ourselves, our children, and our world.

Let us break the chain of darkness and let in the Light.

CHAPTER 26

The Correlation Of Cause And Effect

The applied aspect of science (as distinguished from research) states that once a given question has been answered, then the information found can be used to *predict* and *control* those parts of nature/human behavior which have been studied.

Science, being a source of *information*, can only provide that information. It cannot provide knowledge or wisdom in the application or use of the information discovered.

The fields of morals and ethics can contribute very clear and definite views on how information may be used to build or to destroy.

The information in this book and the references given provides a totally new system for considering: (1) the punishment of adults by other adults when there is victory in war. (The Treaty of Versailles in WW I versus The Marshall Plan in WW II); and (2) the punishment of children by adults in parenting.

If this information is *not applied*, then the situation is one of

GLOBAL HYPOCRISY

"It was a good idea, but we didn't get around to it."

Zaire, Cambodia, Bosnia, and Kosevo are all fine illustrations of the non- or partial application of the system noted above.

CHAPTER 27

Avoiding Future Problems

Children born into our world do not bring with them hate, fear, and the desire for revenge. These personality characteristics are added after they arrive. This is most often done by the parents.

Without the characteristics of hate, fear, and revenge, children will be able to meet the world with maturity, objectivity, and integrity. In this way, an enormous blessing will be brought to our world.

CHAPTER 28

Present Dangers And Parallels Of
Now And The NAZI Era

I. The number of abused children in America is *2.6 million.* The

Schützstaffel at its maximum was *1 million men.*

II. Non-success in removing racial and group tensions.

III. Satanism in America (per TV reports)

IV. Satanism in children in America (per TV reports)

V. Neo-NAZI, ultra-right, militia, hate-based groups (494 per TV news

reports in March 1998)

VI. McCarthy – II possibility.

CHAPTER 29

The Power Of History Versus Understanding

The power of creative understanding can be used to *shape* history to the degree of society's understanding of the forces involved.

This understanding is increased by the lesser amount of child abuse. It is decreased by the greater amount of child abuse. This is due to the individual involvement of each member of society (their survival).

The combination of maximum child abuse and maximum objective difficulty, as seen in Part I, creates a situation of minimum understanding in which organized revenge (the Holocaust) becomes possible. Direction by charisma lights the fuse.

In descriptions of "science", one reads that the object is "prediction and control." Having the understanding that child abuse is the *cause* of crime and violence, it is necessary that this understanding be *applied.* Application means elimination of child abuse.

To *not* apply this understanding means:

1)   hypocrisy

2)   danger

3)   suffering

4)   needless expense

The problem presently faced by society is to gain motivation to *apply* the understanding. All actions taken to apply the understanding will result in a gain and blessing to society. All actions *not* taken will result in needless suffering and difficulty.

There can be no reaction, as revenge, without an action, as abuse. It is essential for the continuation, and indeed for the survival, of our present efforts toward civilization to decrease the number of revengeful actions on our planet. As we have seen, eliminating child abuse is a primary way of doing this. Ever greater urgency is upon us. There is more than one way to produce a Holocaust. It does not have to be by the *mass* determination of revenge. The ever greater sophistication of nuclear, biological, and poison technology, with increasing ease of miniaturization, enables one individual, or a small group, to destroy a city in an instant — or a very short and irreversible time.

The greater the intelligence; the greater the sensitivity. Under the trauma of abuse, the personality can produce a combination of only two fragments: (1) abstract intelligence, and (2) desire for revenge. This combination, in only ONE individual, can produce *immense* destruction.

There is no valid way at present to know who this individual is, or which abused child might become this individual.

So, the *ONLY* way for society to survive is to eliminate child abuse completely.

References Cited In Part IV

1. "The Songs of Chandra Lal" (Tom Pierce)

2. "Ocean Born" by Chris Griscom
    The entire book

3. Lamaze International Water Births
    2025 "M" Street, NW, Suite 800
    Washington, D.C. 20036-3309
    1-877-952-6293
    Hqtrs. 1-800-368-4404

4. "Care of the Soul" by Thomas Moore
    The entire book

5. "Prime References" — List

6. Care for Our Precious Forests
    The Circle of Life Foundation
    P. O. Box 3764
    Oakland, CA 94609
    510-601-9790

7. Care of Whales, Dolphins, and Seals
    The Sea Shepherd
    P. O. Box 628
    Venice, CA 90294-9907
    310-301-SEAL (7325)
    Fax: 310-574-3136

8. Care for Local Animals
    Spay and Neuter
    SPCA's Animal Rescue

9. Little Girls in Pretty Boxes by Joan Ryan. 1995
    Warner Books
    1271 Avenue of the Americas
    New York, NY 10022
    The entire book

10. Investor's Business Daily, May 20, 1996 – Front Page
    Source: National Institute of Justice

11. The local Planned Parenthood Association

Prime References

John Bradshaw

Channel 32 KQED:

34 million children are affected

80% of jail inmates are victims

Progressive generations are involved.

Hitler was a victim

Alice Miller's book – "For Your Own Good"

Revenge – 6 million plus WW II

Journal of Consulting and Clinical Psychology

Volume 49, Pgs. 63-71 – Rosenbaum and O'Leary

Marital violence (all types) is in 60% of all marriages

Physical   ↘ Sexual is a
Emotional   ↗ combination

There is violence in *at least* 15 million marriages.

13% of all marriages or 5 million are *severe*.

It is an area of "selective inattention."

Gayford (1975)

Experiencing *child abuse* or witnessing parental spouse abuse *predisposes* the husband to *follow* the role model, and the wife to *tolerate*.

Get therapy very early in the marriage to decrease abuse. There is alcohol use in 65%.

American Journal of Orthopsychiatry

Volume 51, Pgs. 692-699:

1. Abusers become violent role models.

2. Wife abusers are child abusers Gayford: 54% of abused husbands and 34% of abused wives also abuse their children.

Children of marriages in which the wife is abused are predisposed by:

1. Role modeling

2. Discord and abuse

3. They must cope with the stress of fear of injury to their mother.

4. Fear of their own abuse

5. They are predisposed to be victims.

Long-term adult problems for the next generation. Retrospective studies

68% of abused wives had mothers who were similarly abused.

They are predisposed to repeat.

An assessment for *both* parents shows an 82% correlation.

Journal of Clinical Psychology 42 (1) Pgs. 169-172

Milner and Gold

Screening spouse abusers for child abuse potential.

Descriptive factors of child abusers:

1) Distress

2) Rigidity

3) Child with problems

4) Problems from family and others

5) Unhappiness

6) Loneliness

7) Negative concept of child and *of self*

Low self-esteem

Guilt as self-criticism

Lack of ego-strength

External losses of control

Reactivity

Emotional problems

Ineffective coping and problem-solving skills

Apprehension, tension, anxiety, and instability

Personnel and Guidance Journal

Volume 61 (4), Pgs. 222-224

Ponzetti

Cate

Koval

Internal factors:

I. Learned predisposition toward violence:

1) Maximum in the observed parents.

2) They were abused themselves.

3) They have a tolerant attitude toward violence.

      a.   setting

      b.   affective context

II. They have great alcohol and drug dependency so they avoid personal responsibility.

III. Inexpressiveness

    – They have verbal inexpressiveness of emotional feelings.

    – It is hard for them to identify their emotions.

    – This is their power strategy.

    If inexpressiveness doesn't work – then *violence* comes.

IV. Emotional Dependence *is extreme*.

    Jealousy

    Possessiveness

V. Lack of assertiveness

    Rigid and traditional sex role attitudes.

    Cultural stereotypes associated with aggressive behavior.

    So – violence versus verbal expression.

Bibliography

A Dance Between Flames
By Anton Gill
Carroll & Graf Publishers, N. Y.
1994

American Journal of Orthopsychiatry

Anatomy of Human Destructiveness, The
By Holt, Reinhart & Winston, N. Y.
1973

Bible, The King James Version

Care of Our Precious Forests
The Circle of Life Foundation
P. O. Box 3764
Oakland, CA 94609
(510) 601-9790

Care of the Soul
By Thomas Moore

Care of Whales, Dolphins, and Seals
The Sea Shepherd
P. O. Box 628
Venice, CA 90294-9907
1-310-301-7325

Character Analysis
By Wilhelm Reich
Farrar, Straus & Giroux, N. Y.
1972

First World War, The
By Martin Gilbert
Henry Holt & Co., N. Y.

For Your Own Good
By Dr. Alice Miller
Farrar, Straus & Giroux, N. Y.
1983

History of an Obsession, The
By Klaus Fischer
Continuum Publishing Co., N. Y.

Hitler, A Study in Tyranny
By Alan Bullock
Bantam Books, Inc., N. Y.
1961

Hitler, The Path to Power
By Charles B. Flood
Houghton Mifflin Co.
1989

Journal of Clinical Psychology

Journal of Consulting & Clinical Psychology

Lamaze International Water Births
1-800-368-4404

Little Girls in Pretty Boxes
By Joan Ryan
Warner Books (1995)
1271 Avenue of the Americas
N. Y., N. Y. 10022

Mein Kampf
By Adolph Hitler
Translated by Ralph Manheim

Nazis, The
Time Life Books, 1980

Ocean Born
By Chris Griscom

Personnel & Guidance Journal

Soul Murder: Persecution in the Family
By Morton Schatzman
Random House, N. Y.
1973

Spear of Destiny, The
By Trevor Ravenscroft
Samuel Weiser, Publisher
York Beach, Maine

To Destroy You Is No Loss -
The Odyssey of a Cambodian Family
By Joan Criddle
Anchor Books
Doubleday, N. Y.

INDEX

HISTORY
SOCIOPATHOLOGY
CHILD ABUSE PREVENTION

Tom Pierce, poet and scholar, using as a nom-de-plume his spiritual name "Chandra Lal" from seventeen incarnations ago with a combination of intuition and research has found a way of eliminating war, crime, and violence from our world. These problems began 6,000 years ago with a climatic change in the eastern Mediterranean area. They must be eliminated so that we can transform our world home into the Paradise it is rightly destined to become.